# Anxiety Detox

## Proven Techniques to Relieve Stress and Find Inner Peace

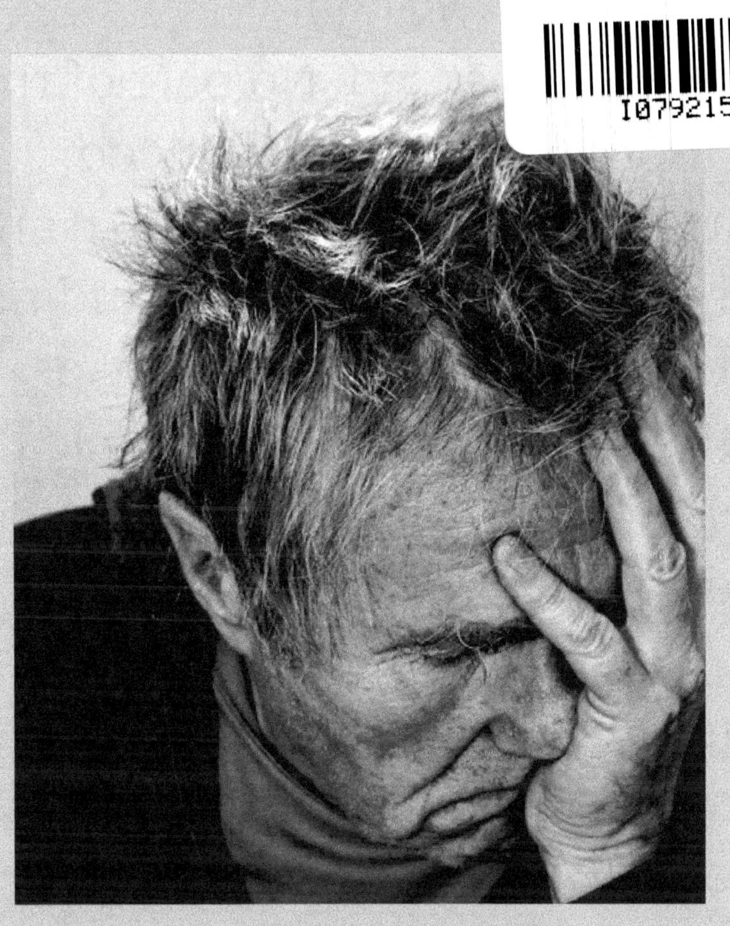

## By: Karan Mangal

# Acknowledgment

This book wouldn't have been possible without the support of my family, friends, and mentors who encouraged me to share my journey. A special thank you to my all mentors for their unwavering belief in my ability to create this work.

I also want to thank you, the reader, for choosing this book. I hope it becomes a source of calm and inspiration in your life.

# Table of Contents

# Introduction
## My Journey to Peace

Let me tell you a story. A few years ago, I felt like I was carrying the weight of the world.

My mind never stopped racing with worries: "What if I fail?" "What if something goes wrong?" This constant overthinking left me drained, scared, and unable to enjoy life.

But here's the thing: I learned how to let go of that fear. It wasn't easy, and it didn't happen overnight, but I found simple steps that changed my life.

If you've ever felt stuck in your own mind, constantly worried or stressed, I want you to know there's hope.

This book will show you proven techniques to take back control, find peace, and enjoy life again.

# Chapter 1: Understanding Anxiety —The Silent Saboteur

Anxiety feels like a storm in your mind, but what is it really?

- Anxiety is your brain's way of protecting you. It tries to warn you of danger, even when there's no real threat.

- You might feel it as racing thoughts, a pounding heart, or even stomachaches.

These are your body's signals that something feels wrong. In this chapter, we'll explore:

- What anxiety looks like: Do you feel nervous, restless, or tense?

- Why it happens: Sometimes, it's from too much stress, a busy lifestyle, or even your diet.

- How to spot it early: Learn to notice your triggers, like certain situations or thoughts that make you anxious.

**The first step to fixing a problem is understanding it. Let's take that step together.**

# Chapter 2: Detoxing Your Mind —Practical Mental Techniques

Your thoughts shape how you feel. If your mind is filled with "what ifs" and doubts, it's no wonder you feel anxious! Here's how you can calm your mind:

- Mindfulness: Focus on what's happening right now, not what might happen later. Start by sitting quietly for one minute and noticing your breathing.

- Breathing exercises: Try this: Breathe in for 4 seconds, hold it for 4 seconds, and breathe out for 4 seconds. Repeat this 5 times.

- Journaling: Write down your worries. Seeing them on paper can help you realize they're not as big as they feel.

- Reframe negative thoughts: When you think, "I'm going to fail," change it to, "I'll try my best, and that's enough."

# Chapter 3: Detoxing Your Body—Caring for Your Physical Well-Being

Your body and mind are connected. If your body feels bad, your mind will too. Here's how to take care of yourself physically:

- Eat foods that calm you: Choose whole foods like vegetables, nuts, and fish. Avoid too much caffeine or sugar, which can make anxiety worse.

- Move your body: Exercise releases chemicals in your brain that make you feel happy. Even a 10-minute walk can help.

- Get enough sleep: Create a bedtime routine. Turn off screens an hour before bed, read a book, or listen to calming music.

- Natural remedies: Try chamomile tea, lavender oil, or magnesium supplements to help your body relax.

# Chapter 4: Detoxing Your Lifestyle—Reclaiming Your Space and Energy

Anxiety thrives in chaos, so let's simplify your life:

- Declutter your space: A clean room can lead to a clear mind. Start by organizing one small area, like your desk or bedside table.
- Set boundaries with technology: Social media and constant notifications can overwhelm your mind. Schedule screen-free times during the day.

- Create routines: Having a daily schedule can make your life feel more predictable and less stressful.

- Choose positivity: Spend time with people who lift you up. Say "no" to things that drain your energy.

# Chapter 5: Stories of Transformation—Real-Life Examples

You're not alone in this. Here are some stories of people who overcame anxiety:

- Sarah's Story: Sarah used to feel sick before every social event. By practicing breathing exercises and setting small goals, she became confident enough to give a speech at work.

- John's Story: John felt crushed by work deadlines. He started using mindfulness apps and now takes 5-minute breaks to breathe and reset.
- Emma's Story: Emma struggled with panic attacks. By journaling her feelings and talking to a therapist, she learned to manage her emotions.

These stories remind us that change is possible. If they can do it, so can you.

# Chapter 6: Your Anxiety Detox Toolkit—Actionable Steps for Change

Here's your step-by-step plan:

- Daily affirmations: Start your day by saying, "I am calm, I am capable, and I am in control."
- Weekly challenges: Try one new anxiety-reducing habit each week, like journaling or a 10-minute walk.

- When anxiety strikes: Use this grounding exercise: Name 5 things you see, 4 things you feel, 3 things you hear, 2 things you smell, and 1 thing you taste.
- Checklist for success:
- Sleep 7-8 hours.
- Drink water.
- Practice deep breathing daily.
- Avoid overcommitting yourself.

# Conclusion: Your Peace Is Within Reach

Anxiety might feel like it's controlling your life, but remember: you have the power to take it back. By using the techniques in this book, you can create a calmer, more peaceful future.

Take it one step at a time. Start with one small change today. You're not alone in this journey, and I'm cheering for you every step of the way.

**Call to Action:**
Take a moment now to pick one exercise from the toolkit and try it. Your new, anxiety-free life is waiting for you—let's start today!

# About the Author

Author is passionate about helping people overcome life's challenges and find peace within themselves. Drawing from personal experience and years of research, Author has dedicated their work to creating practical, accessible tools for anxiety relief.

When not writing, Author enjoys to be around good people, give positivity. You can connect with Author at linkedin.

link: https://www.linkedin.com/in/karanmangal-fullstackdeveloper/

Thanks for ur time!!